National Park Service
U.S. Department of the Interior

Natural Resource Program Center

Northern Elephant Seal Monitoring 2005-2007 Report, Point Reyes National Seashore

Natural Resource Technical Report NPS/SFAN/NRTR—2008/085

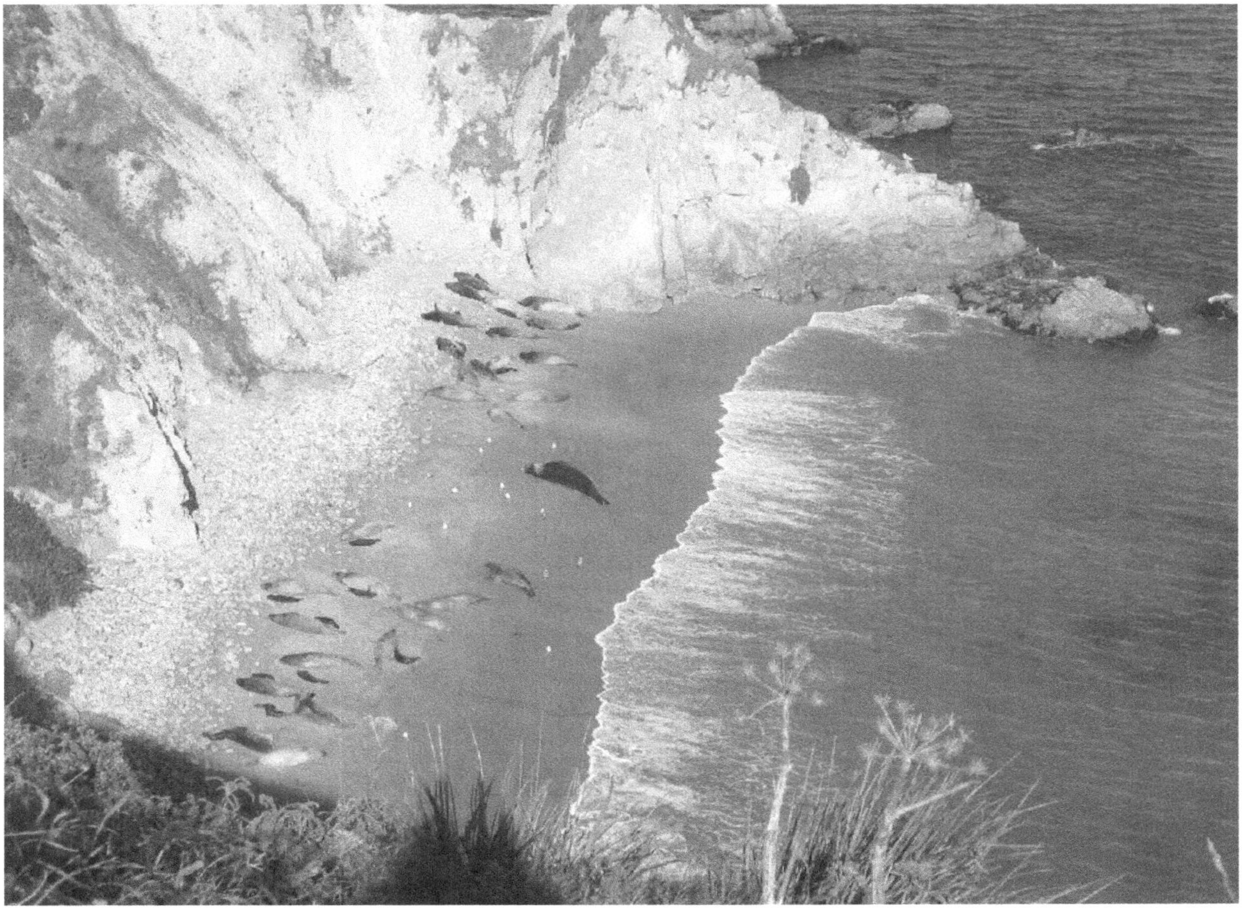

ON THE COVER
Cow and pup pairs with alpha bull male at the Gus' Cove northern elephant seal breeding sub colony in Drake's Bay, Point Reyes National Seashore during mid-January 2007. Photograph by: Kristen Truchinski, Marin Conservation Corps.

Northern Elephant Seal Monitoring 2005-2007 Report, Point Reyes National Seashore

Natural Resource Technical Report NPS/SFAN/NRTR—2008/085

Adams, Dawn
Jensen, Heather
Nevins, Hannah[1]
Truchinski, Kristen[2]
Roberts, Dale
Allen, Sarah

National Park Service
San Francisco Bay Area I&M Network and Point Reyes National Seashore
One Bear Valley Road
Point Reyes Station, California 94956

[1]Moss Landing Marine Laboratory
8272 Moss Landing Road
Moss Landing, California 95039

[2] Marin Conservation Corps
27 Larkspur Street
San Rafael, CA 94901

January 2008

U.S. Department of the Interior
National Park Service
Natural Resource Program Center
Fort Collins, Colorado

The Natural Resource Publication series addresses natural resource topics that are of interest and applicability to a broad readership in the National Park Service and to others in the management of natural resources, including the scientific community, the public, and the NPS conservation and environmental constituencies. Manuscripts are peer-reviewed to ensure that the information is scientifically credible, technically accurate, appropriately written for the intended audience, and is designed and published in a professional manner.

The Natural Resource Technical Reports series is used to disseminate the peer reviewed results of scientific studies in the physical, biological, and social sciences for both the advancement of science and the achievement of the National Park Service's mission. The reports provide contributors with a forum for displaying comprehensive data that are often deleted from journals because of page limitations. Current examples of such reports include the results of research that addresses natural resource management issues; natural resource inventory and monitoring activities; resource assessment reports; scientific literature reviews; and peer reviewed proceedings of technical workshops, conferences, or symposia.

Views and conclusions in this report are those of the authors and do not necessarily reflect policies of the National Park Service. Mention of trade names or commercial products does not constitute endorsement or recommendation for use by the National Park Service.

Printed copies of reports in these series may be produced in a limited quantity and they are only available as long as the supply lasts. This report is also available from the San Francisco Bay Area I&M Network website (http://www.nature.nps.gov/im/units/SFAN) on the internet, or by sending a request to the address on the back cover.

Please cite this publication as:

Adams D., H. Jensen, H. Nevins, K. Truchinski, D. Roberts and Sarah Allen. 2007. Northern Elephant Seal Monitoring 2005-2007 Report, Point Reyes National Seashore. Natural Resource Technical Report NPS/SFAN/NRTR – 2008/085. National Park Service, Fort Collins, Colorado.

NPS D-113, January 2008

Contents

Figures

Tables

Executive Summary

Northern elephant seals (*Mirounga angustirostris*) established a breeding population at Point Reyes National Seashore (PORE) in 1981 after near extirpation from North America. Currently, elephant seals breed at three sites in PORE including Drake's Beach (NDB), Point Reyes Headland (PRH), and South Beach (SB). In response to the increase of the breeding population of seals and associated park activities, PORE began to monitor the elephant seal population to contribute to the understanding of population changes and management needs, and to develop research, interpretation and enforcement strategies.

During December to March of each breeding season, we conducted a complete census a minimum of once per week at all breeding sites. In 2006, 20 complete censuses were done and 26 in 2007. Each season, we applied flipper tags to weaned pups, and conducted weekly surveys to resight tagged animals. Reproductive productivity index was estimated as the number of pups compared to number of adult females.

Using a correction factor, we estimated a total population size of 2,100 and 2,285 seals at PORE in 2005 and 2006, respectively. Almost 50% more females were counted at NDB colony sites in 2006 (223) compared with 2005 (147). There also was a smaller increase of 20% at NDB in 2007 (272). We suspect that due to hazardous coastal weather and tide conditions coinciding with the initial arrival of females, NDB became a more attractive colony site than PRH in 2006. The other colony sites, PRH and SB, showed much smaller increases in numbers of female seals (10% and 20% respectively) in 2006 and declines (-13% and -30%) in 2007, indicating movement from these sites to NDB.

During the 2006 season, a total of 225 elephant seal pups were tagged. In 2007, we tagged 232 weaned pups and two sub-adult males. In 2006, 63 seals were resighted (78 tag observations) with tags originally applied at PORE. In 2007, 78 seals were resighted (103 tag observations) as PORE seals. The highest proportion of seals resighted were females, followed by multiple age classes of males, then yearlings and weaned pups. A total of 36 elephant seals (46 tag observations) originally tagged at other colonies were documented at PORE breeding sites during the 2006 season; and 32 seals (39 tag observations) were resighted during the 2007 breeding season.

The overall population productivity index was 0.82 in 2006 and 0.93 in 2007. Since 2005, there has been a slightly greater increase in productivity at the more recently colonized sites (NDB, SB) compared with the remote PRH site. Reduction of human disturbance through park-implemented signage, increased law enforcement near colonies, a docent program and greater public awareness has likely contributed to the successful establishment of these peripheral sites.

Acknowledgements

The Marin Conservation Corps Americorps Program Members were key partners in the field and data management of the program. Many volunteers contributed to the elephant seal monitoring, including W. Holter (2006-07), S. Waber (2006-07), A. Walker (2006-07), S. Van Der Wal (2006-07), K. Carolan (2006-07), M. Divens (2006-07), T. Schane (2006-07), E. Sojourner (2006-07), E. Brody (2006), M. Galloway (2006), and J. Hall (2006). The Marine Mammal Center continues to be an important partner in marine education and research.

The program received financial support from the NPS San Francisco Bay Area Inventory and Monitoring Network, Point Reyes National Seashore, the David and Vicki Cox Family Foundation, and the Point Reyes National Seashore Association. Thanks also to the PORE Elephant Seal Docent Program volunteers who spend many wintry hours to enthusiastically share the wonders of northern elephant seals to Seashore visitors.

Introduction

After having been extirpated to near extinction at the turn of the century, northern elephant seals (*Mirounga angustirostris*) have re-established breeding colonies on isolated beaches and offshore islands along the California coast since the 1950's (Stewart et al. 1994). In 1981, the first northern elephant seal birth was recorded at an isolated pocket beach at the Point Reyes National Seashore (PORE; Allen et al. 1989). The colony has increased steadily since then, fueled by immigration of mature animals from nearby breeding colonies at Año Nuevo and the Southeast Farallon Islands (Ptak 1992; Adams 1993; Sydeman and Allen 1999, S. Allen unpublished data). By 1992, females born at PORE began to return to pup at their natal rookery (Adams 1993). The colony continued to grow exponentially until 1997, when over 300 pups were estimated to have been produced (Sydeman and Allen 1999). Since 1997, the population growth rate has slowed, but breeding elephant seals have expanded into new colony sites within the Seashore.

Currently, northern elephant seals breed on beaches in three main colonies; Point Reyes Headlands, Drake's Beach, and South Beach, and at several smaller sites around the Headlands and Point Reyes Beach. In response to the increase of the breeding population of seals within the park and associated park activities, the park created a Northern Elephant Seal Management Plan (Allen 1995) to: (1) set guidelines for research, interpretation, and enforcement, (2) contribute to the understanding of population changes and possible further growth and management needs, and (3) to develop research, interpretation and enforcement strategies.

To fulfill these goals, PORE has been monitoring elephant seal population size and productivity during their breeding and pupping season annually since 1995. For the period 2005-2007, the elephant seal population at PORE was monitored through a joint effort of the San Francisco Bay Area Inventory and Monitoring Program (SFAN) and PORE. The objectives of the SFAN Northern Elephant Seal Monitoring Program are to determine long-term trends in annual population size, reproductive success, and annual and seasonal distribution at PORE and to identify potential or existing threats. A more detailed description of the objectives and methods used in the SFAN Northern Elephant Seal Monitoring Program is found in the draft SFAN Pinniped Monitoring Protocol (Hester et al. ms). The methods are outlined in this report to provide context to the reader. This report is a summary of the elephant seal breeding season monitoring program activities and results of the 2006 and 2007 seasons.

Methods

Study Site

Northern elephant seals breed at three sites in the park: Point Reyes Headlands (PRH, a.k.a. main colony), the northern extension of Drake's Beach (NDB), and South Beach (SB, a.k.a. Southernmost section of Point Reyes Beach; Figure 1). These main breeding sites are divided into sub-sites, for more accurate counting. There are seven sub-sites at Point Reyes Headlands: Cove 1 (C1), Cove 2 (C2), Cove 3 (C3), Cove 4 (C4), Tip Beach (TIP), Loser Beach (LB), and Dead Seal Beach (DSB). There are four sub-sites within NDB: North Drakes Beach (NDB), Lifeboat Station (LBS), Gus's Cove (GUS), and Chimney Rock Cove (CRC). At South Beach, there are three sub-sites: Lighthouse Beach (LTH), Nunes Ranch Beach (NUN), and Mendoza Ranch Beach (MEN; Figure 1).

In addition to the breeding sites, park staff and visitors reported elephant seals hauled out on several other beaches in the park (Limantour, Ken Patrick Visitor Center, Kehoe Beach, and Double Point). We compiled these incidental reports, but these data are excluded from the breeding census counts, because they are not systematically surveyed. It is assumed that the breeding site censuses account for the animals (typically sub-adult males and immatures) that move among sites during the breeding season.

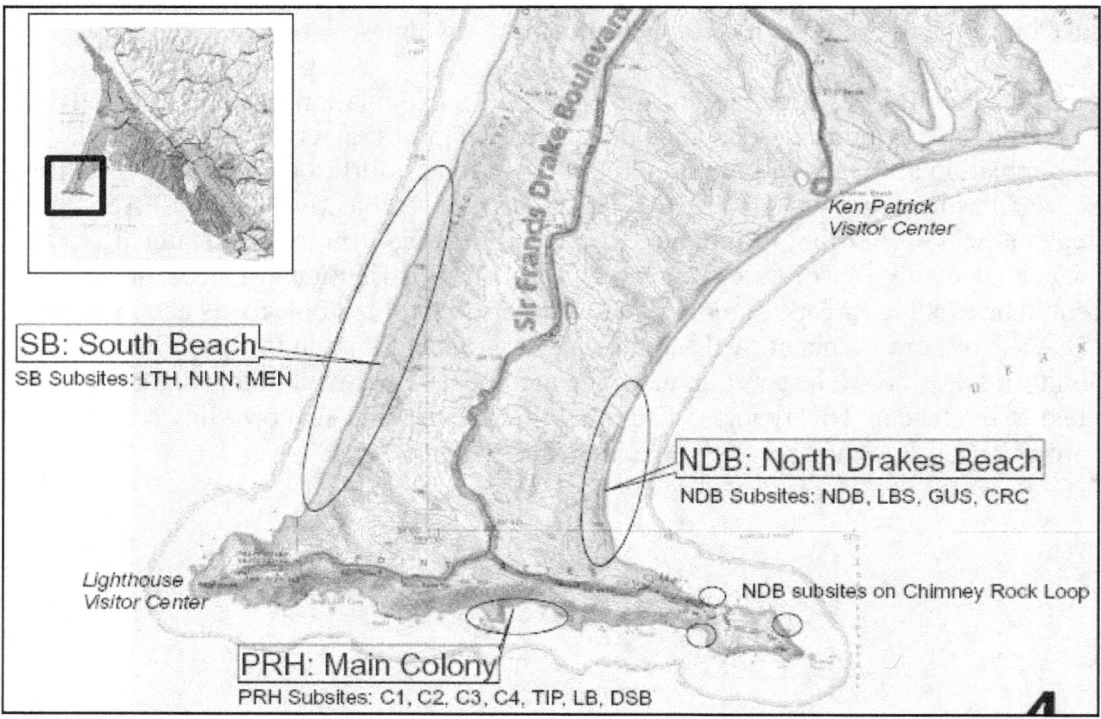

Figure 1. Northern elephant seal breeding sites at Point Reyes National Seashore.

Field Methods

Population and Productivity Surveys

During December to March of each breeding season, we conducted a complete census of elephant seals a minimum of once per week at all breeding sites within the park (PRH, NDB, and SB). During the peak period of pupping from January to the end of February, we conducted two censuses per week to try to capture the peak female and pup/weaned pup counts. We counted seals from fixed vantage points on cliffs with the aid of a 40X spotting scope and 8-10X binoculars. We tallied sex and age groups within each sub-site; adult female (Cow), bull male (Bull), sub-adult male classes 1-4 (SA1-4), immature (IMM), yearling (YRLNG), nursing pup (Pup; including dead pups), weaned pup (WNR). Male age classes are distinguished by the extent of the chest shield, the length of the proboscis, and overall body length (see male aging chart; LeBoeuf and Laws 1994). New observers were trained by experienced observers to judge male age classes in the field.

Because the northern elephant seal breeding season splits the calendar year, in this report the latter year is used to refer to the breeding season (i.e., December 1997 to March 1998 would be referred to as the 1998 season).

Survivorship and Site Fidelity

Individually marking animals allows researchers to estimate survivorship, site fidelity, and emigration rates. Colony-specific tag color and serial numbers allow researchers to track individuals over many years, with the potential to also study individual animal productivity. Similar to the procedures at other northern elephant seal colonies, we applied individually numbered plastic tags (Dalton brand) to the hind flipper of pups born at PORE under National Marine Fisheries Service (NMFS) permits 373-1575 and 373-1868-00.

Until 1998, the number of weaned pups tagged each year roughly approximated the total number of pups surviving to weaning. Due to the high pup mortality and reduced colony access during the 1998 El Niño storm events, only about 27% of the pups produced were tagged. Between 1999 and 2004, approximately 55% to 94% of the pups produced were tagged. Since 2005, the number of pups surviving to weaning has far surpassed the number researchers were able to tag. At PRH, we were no longer able to tag all weaned pups due to restricted access to the colony site for safety reasons and increased density of the breeding seals. At NDB and SB, we tagged the majority of pups with at least one tag. The general goal as outlined in the Draft Pinniped Monitoring Protocol (Hester et al. ms) and NMFS permit was to tag 200-300 weaned pups each year. In future data analysis, we can obtain estimates of survivorship, mortality and immigration from this sample of known-age seals. Here we simply report the number of pups single or double tagged in the cohort of each year. Double-tagging (tagging both hind flippers) is done to estimate tag loss and to increase the chance of resighting an animal, since both flippers are not always visible. At PORE, double-tagging has been done opportunistically only without further plans to estimate tag loss. When possible, we also tagged a few adult males to track inter-site movement.

Surveys to re-sight tagged individuals occurred weekly on the easily accessible beaches (NDB, SB). Re-sight surveys to PRH sites occurred only in December, early January and March because of concerns for human safety. The PRH sites have difficult access, a higher density of seals, and increased seal movement on the beach. We recorded tag information from animals during re-sight surveys. Location of seal, flipper tag number, color, side (left or right), and position among the inter-digit webs (round or square) were recorded for each tagged animal. Also, the presence or absence of tags on the other flipper was recorded. Animals with freeze brand marks (applied at other breeding colonies) and distinctive scars such as shark bites were recorded in the notes field. If the animal was an adult-sized female, we recorded whether she was with a nursing pup, and the pup size class (P1-4). If the animal was a subadult 4 or bull male, we recorded whether it was dominant on the beach (Alpha), sub-dominant (Beta), or not associated with females (NA).

Temporary dye-marking was used in some years to identify individual breeding adults, and to document adult and sub-adult male movement. Dye marks allow individual identification without needing to read the tags each visit during a season. We applied dye-marks with "Lady Clairol, Natural Blue-Black" human hair dye using the applicator bottle. We used a series of individual alpha-numeric codes to dye-mark animals, using the first letter to denote the first site the animal was observed (i.e., "D2" is the second seal marked at the Drakes Beach site). If possible, marks were placed on the back and side of the animal to insure good visibility of the mark from a distance. The orientation and shape of the dye-mark was recorded on a "scar card" to help field staff identify difficult to read dye marks during subsequent observations. The hair dye is innocuous to the seals and the mark disappears after the annual fur molt. In addition, marked males have increased the ability of volunteer elephant seal docents to track individuals from the Elephant Seal Overlook above the North Drakes Beach population and educate park visitors about the monitoring study.

Analytical Methods

Data Management

All data gathered during the breeding season was entered into a Microsoft Access XP database maintained at PORE. The survey data was entered on a weekly basis and the resight and tagging data was entered on a bi-monthly basis. Error checking procedures within the database were used and all data entered were checked against the raw data sheets at the end of the season.

Population Size

Breeding population estimates were based on maximum survey counts for sex and age groups by colony (Allen et al. 1989). During the breeding season, not all age classes are present on the beaches so an accurate total population size was not possible. The NMFS estimates the elephant seal population size by using raw pup counts multiplied by the inverse of expected ratio of pups to total animals based on a paper by McCann 1985 Boveng (1988) and Barlow et al. (1993) recommend using 3.5 as an appropriate multiplier for a rapidly growing population such as the California stock of northern elephant seals. The PORE population estimates were based on the pup count multiplier (3.5) used with the maximum total of pup and weaner counts by colony or sub-site.

Productivity

We used a standardized productivity index similar to the Southeast Farallon Island study (Lee 2006). The index was determined by using the following formula:

$$\frac{\text{Maximum count of weaned pup and pups}}{\text{Adjusted maximum count of females}} = \text{Productivity Index}$$

The index was calculated for colony sites and the population. We estimated the total number of breeding females using the weekly mean - maximum count of adult females during peak pupping (approximately 27 January to 3 February) adjusted by including the adult female counts 33 days prior and 33 days after the peak count for each colony site (Adams 1993; LeBoeuf and Laws 1994; Table 1). This adjustment takes into account females that depart early and those that have not yet arrived at the time of the peak count (average female stay at colony is 6 days prior to pupping + 27 days nursing period; LeBoeuf and Laws 1994). The assumptions of this method to determine productivity are that we are able to capture the high count of pups plus weaners and adult females during the bi-weekly surveys and that female natality is unknown but relatively stable across years. The index reflects productivity only and not mortality (dead pups are included in the total) that occurred at the breeding site.

Survivorship and Site Fidelity

Currently, we are not analyzing the tag resight data collected yearly, but will participate in a future range-wide tag resight analysis with managers and university researchers working at other elephant seal monitoring sites. In previous years we have calculated pup mortality based on the number of weaned pups present at the end of the breeding season divided by the estimated total number of pups born, but we did not calculate this estimate for this report.

Results

Population surveys

We conducted censuses each breeding season at all three primary colony sites (PRH, NDB, SB) from December through March. In 2006, 20 complete censuses were done; in 2007, 26 counts were done. Additional individual sub-site counts were completed during resight surveys, but those counts are not included in these results. Population size and productivity data for 2005 is provided for comparison. Breeding population estimates and productivity index values in Tables 1 and 2 are weighted means calculated from total figures and not simple means of the value for each of the colony site or sub-site.

Table 1. Point Reyes National Seashore northern elephant seal population and productivity counts for 2005 - 2007 breeding seasons at each colony site.

Season	Colony site[1]	Max # of females	Adjusted max # of females[2]	Max # of pups plus weaners	Breeding population size estimate[4]	Overall population estimate[5]	Productivity index[6]
2005	PRH	384	408	320	677	1120	0.78
	SB	29	30	28	73	98	0.93
	NDB	147	166	158	322	553	0.95
	Total	560	604	506	1072	1771	0.84
2006	PRH	413	447	352	768	1232.0	0.79
	SB	30	36	39	99	136.5	1.08
	NDB	223	245	209	463	731.5	0.85
	Total	666	711	600	1330	2100	0.82
2007	PRH	362	387	377	809	1319	0.97
	SB	24	25	24	70	84	0.96
	NDB	272	293	252	551	882	0.86
	Total	658	705	653	1430	2285	0.93

[1] Census includes all sub-sites (e.g. NDB included NDB, CRC, GUS)
[2] The adjusted maximum includes the number of females counted 33 days prior and after the maximum count.
[3] The maximum count of pups plus weaners on a single census for each colony site.
[4] The maximum survey count of all seals.
[5] Based on pup count multiplier of 3.5.
[6] Maximum number of young divided by the adjusted maximum number of females.

Table 2. Point Reyes National Seashore northern elephant seal productivity for 2006 - 2007 breeding seasons at NDB sub-sites.

Season	Colony site	Max # of females	Adjusted max # of females[1]	Max # of pups plus weaners[2]	Productivity index[3]
2006	CRC	24	31	17	0.55
	GUS	50	53	46	0.87
	NDB	150	173	154	0.89
	Total	224	257	217	0.84
2007	CRC	87	90	76	0.84
	GUS	40	40	36	0.90
	NDB	145	154	150	0.97
	Total	272	284	262	0.92

[1] The adjusted maximum includes the number of females counted 33 days prior and after the maximum count for each sub-site.
[2] Maximum count of pups plus weaners at each individual sub-site (different dates).
[3] Maximum number of young divided by the adjusted maximum number of females.

Productivity

The peak number of breeding females (cows) occurred during the last week of January and first week of February in both years, similar to past years (NPS, unpublished data). In 2006, the peak number of females counted at PRH occurred on 01/27/06, at SB on 01/24/06 and at NDB on 01/31/06. In 2007, the peak number of females at PRH was on 1/26/07, at SB on 01/29/07, at NDB on 01/29/07. The first pups were recorded on 12/16/05 and 12/19/06, both at the PRH site. The peak number of pups and weaners (combined counts) was 585 on 02/21/06 and 650 on 02/15/07.

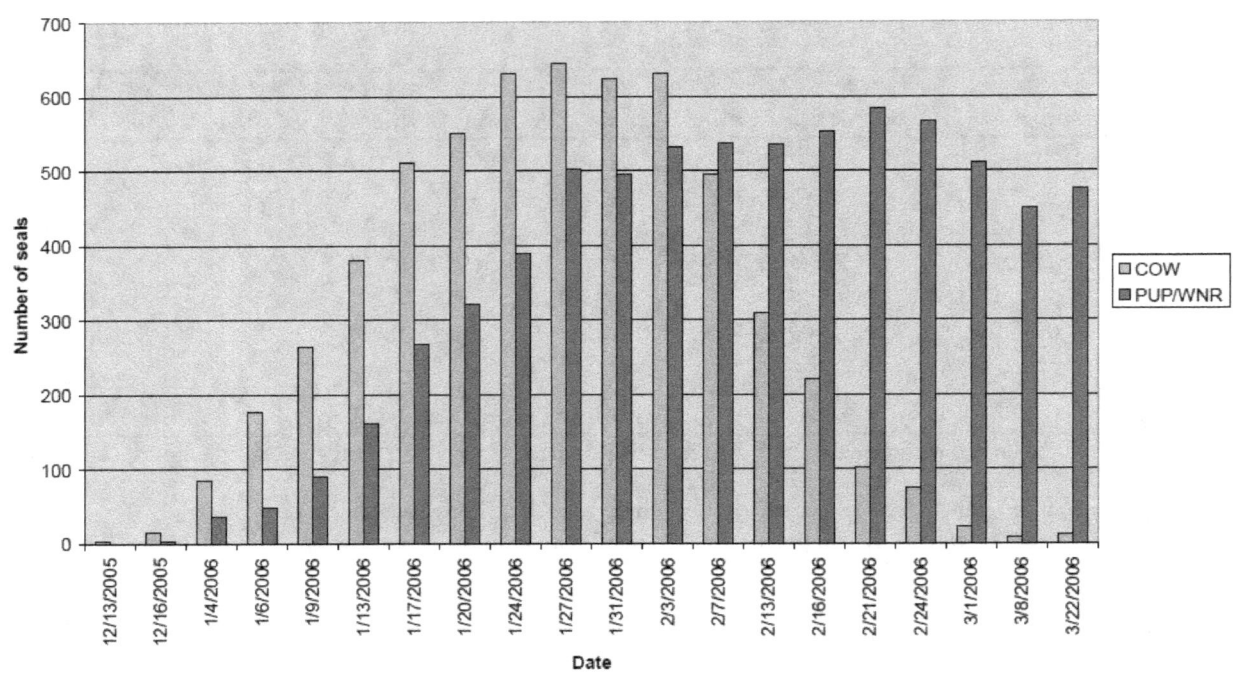

Figure 2. Number of northern elephant seal cows and pup/weaners at Point Reyes National Seashore during the 2006 pupping season by survey date.

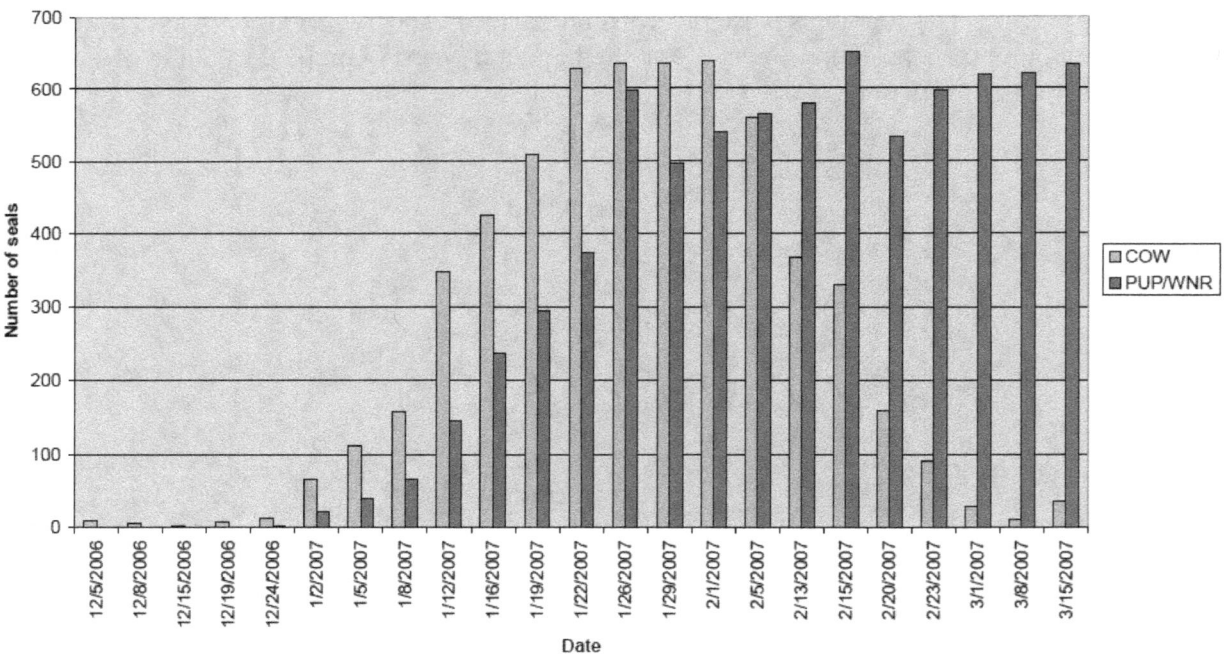

Figure 3. Number of northern elephant seal cows and pup/weaners at Point Reyes National Seashore during the 2007 pupping season by survey date.

Survivorship and Site Fidelity

During the 2006 pupping season, a total of 225 seals were tagged as weaned pups; in 2007, 232 weaned pups were tagged, and two sub-adult males were tagged (Table 3). In both years, approximately 36% of the pups produced were tagged.

Table 3. Number of northern elephant seals tagged at Point Reyes National Seashore by year, age class and sex.

Breeding season		Adult Female	Bull	Sub-adult Male SA4	SA3	Weaner Male	Female	Unknown	Total
2006	Seals tagged	0	0	0	0	68	62	95	225
	Single	0	0	0	0	60	58	90	208
	Double	0	0	0	0	8	4	5	17
	Tags applied	0	0	0	0	76	66	100	242
2007	Seals tagged	0	0	2	0	103	55	74	234
	Single	0	0	2	0	101	55	72	230
	Double	0	0	0	0	2	0	2	4
	Tags applied	0	0	2	0	105	55	76	238

In 2006, biologists did not apply dye-marks to any seals. In 2007, biologists applied temporary dye-marks to 14 seals (7 sub-adult males, 6 bull males, and 1 adult female).

Tag Resighting

The amount of effort expended to resight tags varied among years. The frequency of resight surveys depended on a number of factors including access to sites, size of colony and access to particular animals (i.e., it is easier to read tags of males and yearlings because they are located on the fringe of the colony compared to females), and ratio of animals on the beach.

In 2006, 63 seals were resighted (78 tag resightings) with tags originally applied at PORE. In 2007, 78 seals were resighted (103 tag resightings) as PORE seals. The highest proportion of seals resighted were females, followed by multiple age classes of males, then yearlings and weaned pups.

A total of 36 seals (46 tag resightings) originally tagged at other colonies were documented at one of the PORE breeding sites during the 2006 season; and 32 seals (39 tag resightings) were resighted during the 2007 breeding season at PORE (Appendix A). The majority of seals seen from other colonies came from Año Nuevo (green) and Piedras Blancas (white) tags, but seals were also seen from San Nicholas Island (red), San Miguel/Santa Rosa Islands (yellow), Punta Gorda (purple), Southeast Farallon Islands (pink with different letters), and releases of rehabilitated animals from The Marine Mammal Center (orange).

Discussion

Population Size and Productivity

The first week in January 2006 brought a number of storms and high tides that combined for extreme wave action on the PRH colony sites. We suspect that these environmental conditions, coinciding with the initial arrival of females, caused NDB to be a more attractive colony site in 2006. Almost 50% more females were counted at the NDB colony site in 2006 than in 2005 with a smaller increase of 20% in 2007 (adjusted maximum counts; Table 1). The other colony sites, PRH and SB, showed much smaller increases (10% and 20% respectively) in 2006 and declines (-13% and -31%) in 2007. In 2005, the adjusted maximum count of females at the NDB *sub-site* was 107. In 2006, the high count of females was 150, and in 2007, the number of females remained at that level with a maximum count of 145 at the NDB sub-site (Table 2). Correspondingly at the NDB sub-site, 39% more weaners/pups were counted between 2005 and 2006. In 2005, the high count for pups and weaners was 111 on 2/12/05; in 2006, 154 pups and weaners were counted on 3/01/06; and in 2007, the high count was 150 pups and weaners on 2/20/07 (Table 2). In addition, resight surveys recorded multiple females who in previous years had given birth on the oldest colony (PRH), but in 2006 gave birth and mated at NDB sub-sites.

Early in the 2006/2007 winter, climate forecasters predicted a weak El Niño year which generally produces more extreme storms and rain events on the Point Reyes coast. El Niño/Southern Oscillation (ENSO) conditions can have strong negative effects on the elephant seal productivity and pup survival and the effect can continue over a couple of years. While the 2007 winter was warmer than average based on sea surface temperature records, it was not as strong as the 1998 ENSO event, and the extreme effects seen in 1998 during the elephant seal breeding season did not occur (NOAA 2007). In addition, the productivity for the PRH sites was high in 2007 and exceeded 2006 based on the productivity index (Table 1). The timing of the early January storms noted in 2006 could have also affected the productivity of the PRH sites if females moved to other areas such as NDB sites to pup.

Another change noted in 2007 was a marked increase in the population size of the Chimney Rock Cove (CRC) sub-site (included in NDB sites). In 2006, the maximum numbers of females (unadjusted) and pups/weaned pups was 24 and 17 respectively. In 2007, the maximum numbers were 87 females and 76 pups/weaned pups (Table 2). The sub-site productivity index increased from 0.55 in 2006 to 0.84 in 2007 (Table 2). The productivity index also reflects mortality to some degree, since pups washed out to sea during storms or high tide events early in the season before the maximum count occurs are not counted. CRC has a southern exposure at the Headlands and receives more wave action than other NDB sub-sites, and researchers have noticed an increase in sand deposition at the beach, which could account for the higher population and productivity success. The other, closest NDB sub-site, GUS, had relatively stable productivity values in 2006 and 2007 of 0.87 and 0.90 respectively (Table 2).

NDB as a colony site appears to have a stable productivity between 2006 and 2007 (0.85 and 0.86, respectively; Table 1). But if the adjusted maximum female count, pup/weaner maximum counts and productivity index are calculated on a sub-site by sub-site basis, the resolution shows an overall increase in productivity between 2006 and 2007 across all sites and at specific sub-sites (CRC, NDB). NDB sub-sites are distinct beaches with different aspects, sand accretion, and wave exposure characteristics (Figure 1). These characteristics could be factors in the synchronicity of sub-sites for maximum counts and female arrival dates, which will affect the colony productivity values as compared to the sub-site productivity values. In contrast, SB has less variation, because it consists of only two contiguous sub-sites with breeding females. PRH breeding beaches are also continuous and within a larger cove.

Coastal conditions during the December through February pupping season differed between the two years, with three-month averages for mean sea level, maximum water levels, and highest tide of the month being lower in 2007. The relatively calmer conditions could also have contributed to an increase in the productivity between 2006 and 2007 at the CRC sub-site (0.55 to 0.84) and at the PRH sites (0.79 to 0.97); but, the theory does not account for the similar increase in productivity at the other, more-protected NDB sub-sites. The increase in productivity at more exposed sites is in contrast to the relatively stable productivity at the other colony sites (Tables 1 and 2). At the SB site, the productivity value of 1.08 in 2006 is likely an artifact of the census dates used in the adjustments to the maximum female count since elephant seals rarely give birth to twins. Both 2006 and 2007 (0.96 productivity value) represent very high productivity at the SB colony site.

Environmental Indicator

Elephant seals are atypical of many animals which breed and forage in the California Current Marine Ecosystem because they forage mostly in Alaska and the north Pacific and so are less susceptible to recent perturbations in normal annual upwelling patterns. The 2005 and 2006 upwelling seasons have been characterized as weak while 2007 was a typical year. Elephant seal productivity did not appear to be directly affected by the 2006 upwelling anomaly (Table 1). During 2005 and 2006 there was a delay in the springtime onset of coastal upwelling which resulted in lower than normal primary production and cascading ecological consequences which included the mass abandonment of Cassin's Auklet (*Ptychoramphus aleuticus*) nests on the Farallon Islands and record low recruitment of young-of-the-year rockfishes (Peterson et al. 2006). The immediate mortality effects of ENSO events at PORE and elsewhere have previously been documented when increased storm events wash out and drown pups (Sydeman and Allen 1999). Elephant seals may be less susceptible to and not immediately affected by local environmental change that was observed in auklets or juvenile rockfish in 2006 since elephant seals range widely to forage into the eastern and central North Pacific. Nevertheless, elephant seals can experience a delayed effect from such perturbations because of their longer gestation cycle, and elephant seal females have been documented to skip a breeding cycle following ENSO events. Such a delayed effect may explain the lack of population growth in 2007 at PORE, and explain why many of the female seals that were satellite tagged during the 2006 breeding season at Año Nuevo were not pregnant when they returned the following season, as was noted by a Sonoma State Researcher (D. Crocker, pers. com.). Some investigators are reporting that the delay in onset of upwelling is consistent with predictions of the influence of global warming (Barth et al. 2007). Further monitoring of the PORE population may reveal in future years whether elephant seals are an indicator of large scale oceanographic changes.

Tagging and Tag Resighting

We have not calculated the amount of hours of tag resighting effort, but the majority of resight survey visits are made to the NDB colony sites because of the ease of colony and animal access. Since a greater proportion of tagging activities and resighting of pink and non-pink tags occurred at the NDB sites, there appears to be a greater proportion of tagged females at the site. Because of the higher level of effort at the most accessible sub-site, NDB, some (30% in 2007) resights of pink tagged animals are a subsequent sighting of a previously sighted seal during that season.

Other Research

In early December 2006, a female elephant seal with a satellite tag applied at Año Nuevo was seen in the PRH colony site and a similar event occurred in March 2007 on the CRC sub-site. In both instances, the field staff of Sonoma State University researcher, Dan Crocker, retrieved the tags.

Operational Issues

Safety Issues

The program had no safety accidents over the two seasons covered by this report. We believe that our excellent safety record is due to a number of basic program safety rules. First year field staff typically do not work on a beach near the seals unless accompanied by more experienced staff; no one tags without another person acting as a safety look-out; and before entering onto a beach with seals, field staff discuss the field objectives, timing, and safety plan for that day's beach visit.

In late fall 2006, the renovation of the Lifeboat Station dock was delayed and extended into the fall juvenile elephant seal haul out period and early breeding season. Field staff had to move subadult elephant seals away from the barge and construction operations. Additionally, education of construction workers was necessary on elephant seal behavior, the Marine Mammal Protection Act guidelines, and construction activity restrictions around the seals.

Due to the high numbers of seals on the PRH sites and increased breeding and fighting activity during January and February, we have limited researcher beach access to the PRH sites to December and late February through mid-March. In mid-March, Common Murres (*Uria aalge*) start attending nesting sites at the Point Reyes Headlands, so we minimize visits and the potential disturbance to nesting seabirds in the last two weeks of March. SB and NDB sites continue to be fairly accessible for tagging and resighting activities, though at the NDB sub-site, the increasing population may eventually limit access to the vegetated bluffs behind the NDB. In addition, the CRC sub-site beach has never been visited for tagging or resighting due to cliff access issues. With sloughing hillsides changing access yearly and, sometimes, within a season, access to the CRC beach should be assessed in future years.

Personnel

In all years, approximately the same number of personnel worked on the monitoring program. Two permanent staff (Sarah Allen, Science Advisor, and Dawn Adams, PRNS Monitoring Coordinator) dedicated approximately 10-15% of their time between December and March training other field staff, surveying, tagging, dye-marking and resighting. Heather Jensen, Term Biological Technician, was the lead field staff and completed most surveys, some tagging, resighting, and data management, and in 2007, also did the majority of training of the Americorps Member. In 2006, the Americorps Member started in January and in 2007, the member started in October. The member was dedicated to the project during the breeding season. Once trained, the member worked with program volunteers to complete most of the population surveys and assisted in tagging and tag resighting. The member was responsible for the bulk of the data entry and data/error checking, and working with the I&M Database Manager, Dale Roberts.

Literature Cited

Adams, J. 1994. Status of the Northern elephant seal, *Mirounga angustirostris* (Gill, 1866), breeding at Point Reyes Headlands, California during 1992-1993. Senior thesis. University of California, Santa Cruz, California. 29 pp.

Allen, S. G. 1995. Northern elephant seal management plan for Point Reyes National Seashore. Report to the National Park Service. 35 pp.

Allen, S. G., S. C. Peaslee, and H. R. Huber. 1989. Colonization by Northern elephant seals of the Point Reyes Peninsula, California. Marine Mammal Science **5** (3): 298-302.

Barlow, J., P. Boveng, M. S. Lowry, B. S. Stewart, B. J. Le Boeuf, W. J. Sydeman, R. J. Jameson, S. G. Allen, and C.W. Oliver. 1993. Status of the Northern elephant seal population along the U.S. West Coast in 1992. Administrative Report LJ-93-01. Southwest Fisheries Science Center, National Marine Fisheries Service, La Jolla, CA. 32 pp.

Barth, J. A., B. A. Menge, J. Lubchenco, F. Chan, J. M. Bane, A. R. Kirincich, M. A. McManus, K .J. Nielsen, S. D. Pierce, and L. Washburn. 2007. Delayed upwelling alters nearshore coastal ocean ecosystems in the northern California current. Proceedings of the National Academy of Sciences. 104 (10): 3719-3724.

Boveng, P. 1988. Status of the Northern elephant seal population on the U.S. West Coast. Administrative Report LJ-88-05. Southwest Fisheries Science Center, National Marine Fisheries Service, La Jolla, CA. 35pp.

Hester, M., S. Allen, D. Adams, and H. Nevins. Pinniped long-term monitoring program for San Francisco Area Network of Parks (draft). San Francisco Bay Area Inventory and Monitoring Network, Sausalito, CA. 133 pp.

Le Boeuf, B. J., and R. M. Laws. 1994. Elephant seals. Pages 1-26. *in* B. J. Le Boeuf and R. M. Laws, editors. Elephant seals: population ecology, behavior, and physiology. University of California Press, Berkeley, CA.

Lee, D. 2006. Population size and reproductive success of Northern elephant seals on the South Farallon Islands 2005-2006. Report to U. S. Fish and Wildlife Service Farallon National Wildlife Refuge, San Francisco, CA. 9pp.

McCann, T. S. 1985. Size, status and demography of southern elephant seal (*Mirounga leonina*) populations. Pages 1-17 *in* J. K. Ling and M. M. Bryden, editors. Studies of sea mammals in south latitudes. South Australian Museum, Adelaide, Australia. 132 pp.

McMahon, C., and C. Bradshaw. 2004. Harem choice and breeding experience of female southern elephant seals influence offspring survival. Behavioral Ecology and Sociobiology **55** (4): 349-362.

National Oceanic and Atmospheric Administration (NOAA). 2007. Climate of 2007 El Niño/Southern Oscillation (ENSO). Available from http://www.ncdc.noaa.gov/oa/climate/research/2007/enso-monitoring.html (accessed on 2007-07-23).

Peterson, W. T., R. Emmett, R. Goericke, E. Venrick, A. Mantyla, S. J. Bograd, F. B. Schwing, R. Hewitt, N. Lo, W. Watson, and others. 2006. The state of the California current, 2005-2006: warm in the north, cool in the south. CalCOFI Report **47**:30-74.

Ptak, L. 1992. Status of the Northern elephant seal at Point Reyes National Seashore. Senior thesis. University of California, Santa Cruz, California. 20 pp.

Stewart, B. S., P. K. Yochem, H. R. Huber, R. L. DeLong, R. J. Jameson, W. J. Sydeman, S. G. Allen, and B. J. LeBoeuf. 1994. History and present status of the Northern elephant seal population. Pages 29-48, *in* B. J. Le Boeuf and R. M. Laws, editors. Elephant seals: population ecology, behavior, and physiology. University of California Press, Berkeley, CA.

Sydeman, W. J., and S. G. Allen. 1999. Pinniped population dynamics in central California: correlations with sea surface temperature and upwelling indices. Marine Mammal Science **15**:446-461.

Sydeman W. J., H. R. Huber, S. E. Emslie, C. A. Ribic, and N. Nur. 1991. Age-specific weaning success of northern elephant seals in relation to previous breeding experience. Ecology **72**:2204–2217.

Appendix A

Table 1. Elephant seal flipper tags seen at Point Reyes National Seashore from other sites during the 2006 breeding season.

Date	Sub-site	Maturity	Sex	Left Tag Color[1]	Left Tag #[2]	Left Tag Position[3]	Right Tag Color[1]	Right Tag #[2]	Right Tag Position[3]	Bull/Cow Status	Pup Size	Comments
2005-Dec-14	C3	YRLNG	F	GR	337_	LR	GR	T269	RS			
2005-Dec-14	C3	YRLNG	U	GR	3128	LSB		NS				nursing 2 pups; in 2002 also
2005-Dec-14	C2	YRLNG	U	GR	379	LS		NS				nursing 2 pups
2006-Feb-02	LTH	ADULT	F		NT		GR	L227	R	NU	P3	
2006-Feb-02	LTH	ADULT	F		NT		GR	150_	RR	NP		
2006-Feb-03	NDB	ADULT	F		NT		GR	0194	RR			
2006-Feb-07	NDB	YRLNG	U	GR	3318	L	GR	L174	RRB			
2006-Jan-05	LTH	ADULT	F		NR		GR	S349	RR		P1	Newborn
2006-Jan-08	NDB	ADULT	F		NS		GR	R896	RR			
2006-Jan-08	NDB	ADULT	F		NT		GR	H747	RR	NU	P1	
2006-Jan-13	LTH	ADULT	F		NT		GR	S349	R	NU	P2	
2006-Jan-20	NDB	ADULT	F		NS		GR	K954	R	NU		
2006-Jan-20	NDB	ADULT	F		NT		GR	_194	RR	PG		
2006-Jan-20	NDB	ADULT	F	GR	0421	LRB	GR	NR		PG		
2006-Jan-23	GUS	ADULT	F		NS		GR	1792	RR	NU	P2	
2006-Jan-23	NDB	ADULT	F	GR	0215	LS		NS		NU	P1	small shark bite on back-ooze a little.
2006-Jan-23	NDB	ADULT	F	GR	0944	L	GR	NS		NU		
2006-Jan-23	GUS	ADULT	F	GR	1769	LS	GR	1768	R			
2006-Feb-07	NDB	SA4	M	OR	654_	LRB		NT				
2006-Jan-20	NDB	ADULT	F	PU	901	LS		NT		NU	P3	
2006-Jan-23	GUS	ADULT	F		NS		PU	727	RR			
2006-Feb-03	NDB	ADULT	F		NS		RE	T952	R	NU	P3	

16

Date	Sub-site	Maturity	Sex	Left Tag Color[1]	Left Tag #[2]	Left Tag Position[3]	Right Tag Color[1]	Right Tag #[2]	Right Tag Position[3]	Bull/Cow Status	Pup Size	Comments
2006-Feb-03	NDB	ADULT	F		NS		RE	4361	RR	NU	P4	
2006-Jan-09	NDB	SA3	M		NT		RE	X138	RR			
2006-Jan-23	NDB	ADULT	F	RE	4361	LS		NT		NU	P2	
2005-Dec-14	C2	YRLNG	U	WH	1797	L		NT				
2006-Feb-02	LTH	SA3	M		NS		WH	1185	RR			
2006-Feb-03	NDB	ADULT	F		NS		WH	X307	RR	NU	P3	
2006-Feb-03	NDB	ADULT	F		NS		WH	X251	RS	NU	P3	
2006-Feb-03	NDB	ADULT	F	WH	X802	LS		NS		NU	P3	
2006-Feb-14	NDB	YRLNG	F		NT		WH	T742	RR			
2006-Feb-22	TIP	SA4	M		NT		WH	1185	RR	NP		Also seen at NDB 01/04/06
2006-Jan-09	NDB	ADULT	F		NT		WH	X386	RR	NU		
2006-Jan-20	NDB	ADULT	F		NS		WH	X851	RS	NU		
2006-Jan-20	NDB	ADULT	F		NT		WH	X251	RS	NU		
2006-Jan-20	NDB	ADULT	F	WH	_261	L		NT		NU	P1	
2006-Jan-20	GUS	YRLNG	U	WH	T793	LR		NS		NU		
2006-Jan-23	NDB	ADULT	F		NS		WH	X386	RR	NU	P2	
2006-Jan-23	NDB	ADULT	F		NS		WH	Y724	RS	NU	P1	
2006-Jan-23	GUS	ADULT	F		NT		WH	X668	RR	NU	P1	
2006-Jan-23	NDB	ADULT	F		NT		WH	X307	RR	NU	P1	
2006-Jan-23	GUS	ADULT	F	WH	1448	L		NS		NU		Not confident of left or right flipper
2006-Jan-26	LBS	SA2	M		NT		WH	X874	RR			
2006-Feb-03	NDB	ADULT	F		NS		YE	Y724	RS	NU	P3	

[1] Año Nuevo (GR) Piedras Blancas (WH) San Nicholas Island (RE), San Miguel/Santa Rosa Islands (YE), Punta Gorda (PU), Marine Mammal Center (OR).

[2] An underscore in the tag number refers to an unread digit; no tag present (NT), no tag seen (NS).

[3] The 1st letter refers to the right (R) or (L) rear flipper; the 2nd letter refers to the round (R) or square (S) side of the flipper; a 3rd letter (B) refers to the inner webbing between the digits or bar versus the standard location for tagging in the outermost webbing.

Table 2. Elephant seal flipper tags seen at Point Reyes National Seashore from other sites during the 2007 breeding season.

Date	Sub-site	Maturity	Sex	Left Tag Color[1]	Left Tag #[2]	Left Tag Position[3]	Right Tag Color[1]	Right Tag #[2]	Right Tag Position[3]	Bull/Cow Status	Pup Size	Comments
2006-Dec-28	NDB	YRLNG	U	GR	3590	LSB	GR	3860	R			
2006-Dec-28	NDB	YRLNG	U	GR	T945	L	GR	3686	R			
2007-Feb-06	NDB	YRLNG	U	GR	3838	LS		NT				
2007-Feb-23	NDB	YRLNG	U		NS		GR	3839	RS			
2007-Jan-08	NDB	ADULT	F		NT		GR	H747	RR	NU	P1	
2007-Jan-15	GUS	ADULT	F		NS		GR	_141	R		P1	
2007-Jan-15	GUS	ADULT	F	GR	1769	LS	GR	NS				Also seen at GUS 01-Feb-07
2007-Jan-17	NDB	ADULT	F		NS		GR	R896	R		P1	Also seen at NDB on 08-Jan-2007
2007-Jan-17	NDB	ADULT	F	GR	2117	LS		NS			P2	
2007-Jan-23	NDB	ADULT	F	GR	0215	LR		NS		PG		Also seen at NDB on 06-Feb-2007
2007-Jan-23	NDB	ADULT	F	GR	NR	L	GR	K954	RS		P3	
2007-Mar-02	LTH	SA2	M	GR	1325	LSB		NT				
2007-Jan-17	NDB	ADULT	F	OR	_53_	LRB		NS			P2	
2006-Dec-18	NDB	BULL	M		NT		PK	D860	RR			
2006-Dec-28	NDB	YRLNG	U	PK	G36	LR	PK	G270	RR			
2006-Dec-28	NDB	YRLNG	U	PK	G36	LR	PK	G270	RR			
2007-Jan-31	LTH	ADULT	F	PK	NR	L	PK	E601	RR	PG		Farallones tag - drilled
2007-Jan-23	NDB	ADULT	F		NT		RE	4361	RS		P2	
2006-Dec-28	NDB	BULL	M		NT		WH	1185	RR			
2007-Feb-01	GUS	ADULT	F	WH	T08	LS	WH	NT			P3	
2007-Feb-06	NDB	ADULT	F		NS		WH	X281	RR	NU	P2	
2007-Feb-06	NDB	ADULT	F		NS		WH	X251	RS		P2	
2007-Feb-06	NDB	ADULT	F		NT		WH	X307	RS		P3	Also seen at NDB on 23-Jan-2007
2007-Feb-13	NDB	ADULT	F	WH	X54	LS		NS				
2007-Jan-12	LTH	SA3	M	WH	X279	LS		NS				Also seen at LTH 02-Mar-07
2007-Jan-15	GUS	ADULT	F		NT		WH	X6	RR		P2	

Date	Sub-site	Maturity	Sex	Left Tag Color[1]	Left Tag #[2]	Left Tag Position[3]	Right Tag Color[1]	Right Tag #[2]	Right Tag Position[3]	Bull/Cow Status	Pup Size	Comments
2007-Jan-15	GUS	ADULT	F	WH	T_08	L		NT			P2	
2007-Jan-15	GUS	ADULT	F	WH	X50	LS		NT		PG		
2007-Jan-17	NDB	ADULT	F	WH	125	LR		NS		PG		
2007-Jan-17	NDB	ADULT	F	WH	1281	LS		NS			P1	
2007-Jan-23	NDB	ADULT	F	WH	X116	LS		NS			P3	
2007-Mar-15	C2	ADULT	F	WH	X89	LS		NS		NU	P4	
2007-Jan-15	GUS	ADULT	F		NT		YE	X838	RR	NU	P1	Female has eye missing - looks like a fresh injury
2007-Jan-23	NDB	ADULT	F		NS		YE	Y125	RR			Also seen at NDB on 06-Feb-2007

[1] Año Nuevo (GR) Piedras Blancas (WH) San Nicholas Island (RE), San Miguel/Santa Rosa Islands (YE), Southeast Farallon Islands (PK with different letters), Marine Mammal Center (OR); an underscore in the tag number refers to an unread digit.

[2] An underscore in the tag number refers to an unread digit; no tag present (NT), no tag seen (NS), tag seen but not read (NR).

[3] The 1st letter refers to the right (R) or (L) rear flipper; the 2nd letter refers to the round (R) or square (S) side of the flipper; a 3rd letter (B) refers to the inner webbing between the digits or bar versus the standard location for tagging in the outermost webbing.

NPS D-113, January 2008

www.ingramcontent.com/pod-product-compliance
Lightning Source LLC
Chambersburg PA
CBHW080939290526
45795CB00007BA/2825